100 LAWS
FOR SUCCESS
AND HAPPINESS

The Life you always wanted and more starts TODAY!

Israel Johnson
"The Motivational Speaker of The Millennium"

Outskirts Press, Inc.
Denver, Colorado

The opinions expressed in this manuscript are solely the opinions of the author and do not represent the opinions or thoughts of the publisher. The author represents and warrants that s/he either owns or has the legal right to publish all material in this book.

100 Laws for Success and Happiness
The Life you always wanted and more starts TODAY!
All Rights Reserved.
Copyright © 2008 Israel Johnson "The Motivational Speaker of The Millennium"
V 4.0 R1.0

This book may not be reproduced, transmitted, or stored in whole or in part by any means, including graphic, electronic, or mechanical without the express written consent of the publisher except in the case of brief quotations embodied in critical articles and reviews.

Outskirts Press, Inc.
http://www.outskirtspress.com

ISBN: 978-1-4327-2595-2

Outskirts Press and the "OP" logo are trademarks belonging to Outskirts Press, Inc.

PRINTED IN THE UNITED STATES OF AMERICA

Table of Contents

INTRODUCTION xi

CHAPTER 1] WHAT IS HAPPINESS AND SUCCESS? 1
   The First level of Consciousness to having Happiness and Success [Knowledge]

CHAPTER 2] WHAT R.O.L.L. MUST I PLAY IN ORDER FOR ME TO LIVE HAPPY AND BE SUCCESSFUL? 5
   The Second level of Consciousness to having Happiness and Success [Learn..Learn]

CHAPTER 3] "I FOUGHT THE LAW AND THE LAW WON" WRITTEN BY SUNNY CURTIS 11

[AUDIO-CD VERSION STARTS HERE]

**CHAPTER 4] IN THE BEGINNING AND END,
"I AM SPIRIT FIRST"** 15

[SPIRIT 17 LAWS]

Law #1] Find your God

Law #2] Make up your mind which God you will serve

[The God that is or the God that you want to be God]

Law #3] You must learn the Character of your God

Law #4] You must have a honest and truthful relationship with your God

Law #5] Your God must possess the 7 necessities needed for you to serve that God

Law #6] Your spirit must serve as a General and Director over your soul and body.

Law #7] A Spirit God will require Spirit-Filled Worship of its Deity

Law #8] The spirit of a person must be developed through the word of a Spirit God

Law #9] You must have a Spirit Guide

Law #10] Your Spirit Guide must have three character traits.

Law #11] Always be conscious that you are connected to the Universe and know that the Universe is one with you.

Law #12] Command your vision to come forth

Law #13] Find a place of regeneration

Law #14] Understand the difference between Purpose, Vision and Destiny

Law #15] Overcome the fear of death

Law #16] Love is an action

Law #17] The voice of reasoning is the enemy of your spirit

CHAPTER 5] SOUL [19 LAWS] 29

Law #1] Find your self

Law #2] Have a management system in place to control your emotions

Law #3] You are what you see and what you hear

Law #4] Find a place of rest for your soul

Law #5] Do not trust your emotions to decide your future

Law #6] Confess your sins to God, not to man

Law #7] Write it down

Law #8] Know your starting 5 [Parent, Teacher, Pastor, Community leader and Self]

Law #9] Choose your friends, don't let them choose you

Law #10] Laugh at yourself

Law #11] Expectation causes Disappointment

Law #12] Yes it can happen to you

Law #13] Cleanse your emotions of self-hatred

Law #14] Forgive yourself with a purpose in mind and let go of the past

Law # 15] Let go of the need to judge

Law #16] Sticks and Stones will break bones, but words will kill you

Law #17] Images, Pictures, and quotes create the environment of success

Law #18] A good attitude comes out of balanced emotions

Law #19] Change your Vocabulary

CHAPTER 6] BODY [15 LAWS].. 41

Law #1] The value of your body must be realized

Law #2] Exercise does more for you than make you sweat

Law #3] Stretch your muscles to unify your body

Law #4] You are made of water

Law #5] Find a family doctor

Law #6] Take control of the times you eat

Law #7] Eat in Moderation

Law #8] Join others that want to improve in their body

Law #9] Rest your body

Law #10] Pray and ask your God to help you in maintaining your health

Law #11] Train the mind, don't let it train you

Law #12] Personal Hygiene plays a big part in being happy

Law #13] Are you storing food or using food?

Law #14] Supplements are needed in today's society

Law #15] Food can become a drug to you

CHAPTER 7] MINISTRY [18 LAWS] 53

Law #1] What is your ministry? You are here to elevate others.

Law #2] The law of help- you cannot help anyone who is not ready to be helped

Law #3] Go where you are needed, not just hired

Law #4] Learn from someone you respect, not just someone you admire

Law # 5] Your ministry is a lifestyle, not a 9 to 5

Law # 6] Learn to deal with people

Law #7] Understand what Self-definition means

Law #8] Are you blessed or just lucky?

WHAT ARE YOU HERE TO DO??[THE 4 IF'S]

Law #9] If you are willing to do it for free….

Law #10] If you are willing to risk your life…

Law #11] If you are willing to let go of all your material belongings…

Law #12] If you are willing to let go of your family and friends….

Conquer "the 4 ifs" and you will find your ministry

Law #13] There is no great reward, without great sacrifice

Law #14] Stay ready and prepared for your BIG OPPORTUNITY

Law #15] Do not despise small beginnings

Law #16] Geographic repositioning is necessary

Law #17] Don't try to solve EVERY problem at your job or you will become the problem

Law #18] Dress for Success

CHAPTER 8] MARRIAGE [16 LAWS] 67

Law #1] Love and Care for Your Self first, before you attempt to love and care for someone else

Law #2] Know what your personal moral code is, you live by

Law #3] Sometimes you can be right and still be wrong

Law #4] The promises you make, reveal your character when they are tested

Law #5] Talk to yourself or write down how you feel about real challenges in your life [THIS TRANSLATES TO HOW YOU WILL COMMUNICATE IN MARRIAGE]

Law # 6] Find the time to celebrate others

Law # 7] Never make a career decision behind someone you are dating

Law #8] Get mad and then get over it

Law # 9] Be careful who you let into your personal life

Law #10] "Just because you are making a good living, it does not mean you are living good"

Law #11] You have a right to good sex

Law #12] Prepare children for life, not to be your drug for you not living life

Law #13] Why have children, if you can't afford them?

Law #14] Who married who? Did you marry the person or

did the person marry your family?

Law #15] The person you're married to will change

Law #16] Empower your spouse

CHAPTER 9] MONEY [15 LAWS].....................................81

Law #1] Knowledge and Understanding of money is better than having money itself

Law #2] Money is generated through your mind and heart

Law #3] Money is the god of things

Law #4] Money cannot be your God if you want true happiness and success

Q: When is money your God?

Law #5] If you want money, get around people who know and understand how money works

Law #6] Understand the difference between getting rich, having prosperity and being wealthy and living poor [learning this LAW will give you the big picture]

Law# 7] Control your money by controlling your emotions

Law #8] Your credit report is your greatest resource to get resources

Law #9] Implement the "three collective practices" in your business life to create an environment of wealth and prosperity

Law #10] Talk to your money

Law #11] Never lend money to friends, if you hope to it back

Law #12] important business relationships are more important than money

Law #13] Rainy days are coming, always have an umbrella

Law #14] Pay your bills

Law #15] Be a giver

CHAPTER 10] ARE YOU QUALIFIED TO CHANGE? 97

The third level of Consciousness for happiness and success.

[Practice..Practice..Practice]

[AUDIO-CD ENDS HERE]

CHAPTER 11] DO YOU HAVE THE AUDACITY TO LIVE HAPPY AND BE SUCCESSFUL? WHO DO YOU THINK YOU ARE? 111

The fourth level of Consciousness to truly have happiness and Success.

[Live..Live..Live..Live]

CHAPTER 12] The Decree and Declaration Over Your Happiness and Success, STARTS TODAY!.. 115

INTRODUCTION
100 LAWS FOR SUCCESS AND HAPPINESS IN THIS LIFE

After 36 years of living this life, "I" personally have struggled to find what happiness and success was and how it was essential to my life and how I defined it myself. I have experienced power, money and excess and I have found it to be temporary. I went to school and got a Master's Degree against all odds and I have found that education is enriching, but yet not needed to be happy or successful. I have witnessed and participated in the world of "fun sin", and still I have found myself wanting. Years have taught me, what I describe at the present as "sound wisdom", that is, what I know now to be real and it is the definition that has given me the courage to live **consistently** happy for the last three years of my life and experience what I discern now to be constant success.

My approach to the conquest of the most sought after understanding of all human beings; is my attempt to share with you, *the questions that haunt you????* The thought or thoughts that have pushed you beyond your own strength.

What are those questions and thoughts that haunt you? It is that which you know you must triumph over in order to precede to the next altitude. Which brings me to the coveted desire, I have for you. I push for you to possess and overcome the hope of accepting the purpose of this life and how we as humans, are subjected to perpetual pain, untimely disappointments and life altering failures that are a lot of times not by our own doing, Yet life demands that we do three unthinkable things and that is; take responsibility of living this life, Define what happiness and success means to us as individuals and practice the core values or LAWS that are needed to live in our own happiness and success.

Great happiness and empowering success is within reach of reality within your life. It is needed for anyone who desires to justify a past of undeveloped potential. Hungered after by individuals living in confusion of where their life is headed now and coveted as a cold glass of water on a hot summer day.

Do you know that you deserve to be happy? Are you aware

of the possibilities that life intended for you and how life itself understands your bitterness, guilt and damaged ambitions? As a matter of fact, it is with your pain of living this life; that now is the time for you not only to be truly happy, but also for you to live in that happiness within a perpetual state, regardless of what happens from this day forth.

Wow! Now at this point either something is about to be imparted into you from this book or the author is simply trying to sell you a dream and pile on the confusion of stress and failure by painting idealistic and unreachable practices that would truly convert into contentment. The encompass of what it takes to have real success and true happiness is your ability to know that everything within the earth and outside of the earth operates within a system of rules, regulations, policies and procedures. There is no such thing as a free spirit. We are all; rather human, animal, moon, stars, plants or any and all things created are governed by rules, regulations, policies and procedures. That's right my friend, you live within a system that was created before you arrived and it will be here long after you're gone. It is with this **first level of consciousness** [*there are 4 levels*] of being happy and successful, that you begin to dust off the haziness of your perception of living this life.

But, with this startling revelation comes the question of why are you here? Why have you been given an extension in life? Even when living either does not make sense or has simply come to the point within you that the value of living has been minimized by the twinge and depression of living? Is it possible that you have expensed yourself to the point of emotional bankruptcy in order for everyone around you to perceive you as "successful" "got it all together" or "you're the one that bounces back from whatever life has thrown at you". Could the truth be that life has become so unbearable that the facade has become the breeding ground for internal hatred, suicidal thoughts, nervous breakdowns, anxiety attacks, multiple prescriptions, uncontrollable desires and consuming fears?

If allowed this book or impartation of sound doctrine will give you the enhanced foundation needed to stand and face the oppositions that will continually attempt to sift you as wheat, help you to overcome the appointed assassins in your life and give you the tools that are needed to live in a joy that literally will elevate you to the point that you will feel like you saunter five feet off the ground.

CHAPTER 1
What Is Happiness And Success?

Say it now and say it loud, "I WILL BE HAPPY AND SUCCESSFUL ALL THE DAYS OF MY LIFE, FOR NOW I WILL KNOW AND SEE CLEARLY WHAT HAPPINESS AND SUCCESS REALLY IS. What is happiness? What is success? Oh many people have danced around both questions, but few have been able to give happiness and success a basis on which a universal person can take, apply and make it their own. But now all of that will change forever in your life. Happiness has been misconstrued as an outward presentation that is affirmed by people we are exposed to or the people we seek to appreciate our ability to live up to other people's interpretation of what it is and how it should be applied to our lives. What a lie! It is the #1 lie told, marketed, and perpetrated that is a complete fabrication of living in a matrix of falsehood and unfulfillment of your time in the earth. *You cannot live for others; you must live for yourself by taking responsibility for yourself.* You are uniquely made and created to task in a very specific function within the universe and without understanding your own entity needs for contentment you are separated from the greatest love of all, **You loving you from within.**

With that being identified, happiness is defined as your ability to manage and balance the six Responsibilities Of Living this Life [R.O.L.L.]. While, Success is measured by your willingness to live in moments of fulfillment that are given to you daily through the six Responsibilities of Living Life [R.O.L.L.]

Success is not fame, fortune, a big car or a bigger house. Celebrities confirm everyday to us that it is the "2nd biggest lie ever sold". Better yet, maybe you come from a family where the availability of "things" were plentiful, but the absence of fulfillment seems to somehow have overshadowed all the things that you were given. Why? You are much more than what you possess. But, somehow and someway the lie of recognition from others and the ability to be associated with corporate products has created this false illusion to the masses that this is what success is and what one must strive for. The other psychological trap of deceptive success is the desire to achieve an objective, rather than to live in the process of the objective. Haven't you seen it before? The successful businessman that sacrifices his health, family, and friends to start a company; only to find out that after he has started the company and the business has brought him money, power and recognition; he hates his life and blows out his brains. Would you call that success? Happiness and Success is yours for the taking and all you have to do is play your part in the big play of life. Yes, you have a **R.O.L.L.** [Responsibilities Of Living Life] to play and your ability to train, develop and focus your attention on your **R.O.L.L.** is going to determine the level of unexplainable happiness and genuine success that you experience in your everyday life.

CHAPTER 2
What R.O.L.L. Must I Play In Order For Me To Live Happy And Be Successful?

Do you know that every day you are judged by the most brutal judge known to man? Do you know who this all-powerful being is that minimizes your ability to be happy when you violate the six responsibilities? The one who's verdict can stop you from getting up in the morning to face the world! It's YOU!!. If you have not come into the reality of who YOU are yet, let me help YOU.

YOU are composed of the three separate beings operating in one unison. You are first **spirit** [*that which gives you life; it is your command center*]. Second, you have a **soul**. [*that which gives you consciousness, emotions, the ability to reason, to learn, to remember, to store information, and to feel* *what other people feel.* Third, you are **body**, *[the physical image and reflection of what is going on in the spirit and soul of a person, it is the part of you that will rise to it greatest potential and just as fast begin to dissipate back to the earth from where it came]*

You are responsible for all three beings! They are you and you are they. If any one of them is ignored, non-validated or seen as unimportant, they will attack the other beings or try to get the other parts of you to compensate for the lack of attention to them. Now, it is impossible for either to compensate for the other, for you must know and understand that each one has an assignment in your life, but you control how they fulfill that assignment. You are 100% responsible for the health of your spirit, soul and body. It was assigned to you before you came into the earth. Therefore it is you that must manage and balance these internal responsibilities to begin the process of true happiness and unbelievable success. If you do not buy into the first three Responsibilities Of Living Life **[R.O.L.L.]** the other three will have no value whatsoever. So please don't take for granite the importance of you taking care of YOU.

·

Now that, half of the foundation has been established we are one step closer to beginning the healing process within the decentralized life style you have lived up to until this point. The next step or the other half of the six Responsibilities Of Living Life **[R.O.L.L.]** is to know that you are also responsible and will be held accountable and judged by how you manage the 3 M's [Your Ministry, Your Marriage, and Your Money] or the other 3 components that collectively equal the 6[Spirit, Soul, Body, Ministry, Marriage, Money] responsibilities of living life [R.O.L.L.].

What are the 3M's you ask? One is **Your ministry. Your ministry** is much more than what you ideally perceive it to be. It is not just the preacher that preaches in a church or the missionary that travels overseas to feed the homeless. Your ministry is your purpose for being here. The vision that you see yourself being a part of and the destiny that was predestined before you where even born. WHAT ARE YOU HERE TO DO? What is the occupation, job or career that you are gifted, skilled at and love to do? You must fulfill your destiny. You must find what you are here to do.

Second is your **marriage. Your marriage** is not just saying; "I do" to someone you love. But, it is at its root, the covenant or promises you have made to yourself. It is the moral code of being responsible and accountable. The promise to love, forgive and understand yourself first and the willingness to keep it real with the person you look at in the mirror daily. You can only attract what you really are. Becoming comfortable with yourself and establishing your personal identity is crucial to your happiness and success in life.

Of course, the third one is your money. **Your money** tells the story of your ability to manage the one thing that is a threat to your <u>relationship with God</u>. It tells the chronicle of a busted character trait, undeveloped business mind, unmanageable life style and the need to justify your existence. It also is your legacy in which your offspring will be measured with to rather you did what was right with the money you had while you lived in the earth.

And there you have it, Happiness! You now have the ability to manage your life in six areas of responsibility. Now you're ready to smile and live happy every after right? **Now comes the second level of consciousness.** Just because a person knows that everything in the earth operates by rules, regulations, policies and procedures, still does not exempt them from complete and utter failure, grief and misery in life. This is why you must get to the 2nd level of consciousness. The **second level of consciousness** says you must know what the rules, regulations, policies and procedures are before you can play the game of life. That is the focus of where we are going next and that is to give you rules, regulations, policies and procedures or LAWS that are needed for you to be purposefully happy and undeniably successful in what I have defined as the six areas of your life that you must focus on in order to experience the daily happiness you deserve and the success that is measured only by your state of consciousness.

success. Happiness is a learned behavior and if it is learned, than you can learn how to be happy.

It is time for you to live by a code of happiness and a peace that lives within your success. It is time to be trained and developed in how joy, love and balance have all been waiting for you to come to the mountain and breathe into your being the fresh air of real happiness and everlasting success. But even when climbing the mountain to get to the top, you need to dress the part, have on the right shoes, be aware of the snakes, rocks, and bears and be aware of how you need to move within the area. Within the Six Responsibilities Of Living Life **[R.O.L.L.]** I will teach you Laws that will govern, protect and enhance your Inner Joy and your defined Success. They will be laws that I will give my life for exchange of them and these 100 laws that will be integrated within the Six [Spirit, Soul, Body, Ministry, Marriage, Money] Responsibilities of Living Life [R.O.L.L.] will revolutionize how you think, feel and live your life. These 100 LAWS will need your respect, honor and practice of them in order for YOU to pursue, maintain and live within the prosperity of your own life. So Now, Right Now, Open your mind and receive in your heart, empowerment for your peace and revelations for your success, for now is your time to live with excitable passion and eagle flying success. For today I give to you 100 Laws for Success and Happiness.

CHAPTER 3
"I Fought The Law And The Law Won" sung written By Sunny Curtis

What is the difference between Michael Jordan and the Chicago street ballers that have equal or greater talent them him? What is the difference between the person who gets pulled over for speeding and the one that was not speeding? What is the difference between happiness and sadness or success and failure? The answer is the person who understands how to play within the rules, boundaries or laws. In addition it is the person that understands that the rules, boundaries or laws are put in place to reward those that embrace them and to punish those that transgress against them is the difference. *Those who have mastered the art of the systems of life and codes of self-elevation only continually experience perpetual happiness and genuine*

[AUDIO-CD VERSION STARTS HERE]

YOU are first **spirit**

[*That which gives you life;*

it is your command center].

IN THE BEGINNING AND END, "I AM SPIRIT FIRST"

CHAPTER 4
SPIRIT
17 LAWS

KJV: God is a Spirit: and they that worship him must worship him in spirit and in truth **[John 4:24]**

KJV: God created man in His own image, in the image of God created he him; male and female created he them.
[Genesis 1:27]

Law#1] Find your God

Without the seeking of an eternal present God, that is supreme in all things, you will defeat the plan of life and fall far short of what your life was created for. You are not your own. Someone is controlling you beyond this world. Why? You are spirit first and your spirit has ruling authority over your soul and body or **should have or is suppose to have??** It is the part of you that will cause sickness in the body and dogma in the soul if it is not connected to its Creator. Your spirit is your Command center. Recognize its power and authority in your life. It is from your spirit that you decree, declare and speak things into existence. But, without the God that created your spirit, your spirit power is diluted and watered down. Find your God and Find Him or Her Today!

Law #2] Make up your mind which God you will serve [The God that is or the God that you want to be God]

The God that is, is the God that has existed, is existing and will exist in the future rather you serve him or her now or never. The God that you want to be is the person or people, places or things that you see, that you have asked to justify your existence, make you feel happy, and the thing that you will manipulate, rob, steal and kill to hold on to. Find and serve an Eternal God or continue to serve people, places and things.

Law #3] You must learn the Character of your God

To know the character of your God, gives you the knowledge to know who you must emulate and what similarities their must be between you and your God. In addition, the character of a God must be balanced. That means support as well as discipline. A God's support should be constructed of grace, mercy and love as well as correction, judgment and hard truths. This is the wisdom of a God and it is this wisdom within your character that will cause you to make better decisions and avoid long-term failures. Have the character of your God.

Law #4] You must have a honest and truthful relationship with your God

If your God is truly God, surely you must have the freedom to be honest and tell the truth. Without it, your God is partial and waiting for you to say things that he can use against you. Your God must be omnipotent. That means your God can see your mistakes and failures before you make them, so therefore if you cannot be honest with your God, your God is a God that fails to see that you will not always agree with Him and your God fails to see that you are not God, but human.

Law #5] Your God must possess the 7 necessities needed for you to serve that God

1. Forgiveness-If it is an all-powerful God, without forgiveness he or she will destroy you
2. Love-Humans need love, like fish need water and if you were created out of strife, than how can you ever be happy?
3. Power- why would you need a God that cannot do

things beyond your own strength?

4. Saviour-He must possess the willingness to save and protect you from the darkness of yourself and the pressure of living in this world
5. Mercy- He must be able to see your faults and not judge you, because when the world has condemned you, you need someone beyond this world, who is still on your side
6. Grace-he must realize that standing next to him; you are stupid, a feeble sheep that will run your head into the wall 100 times before you get it right.
7. Shepherd- he must be a leader that you can trust with your spirit, body, soul, money, ministry, and marriage.

Law #6] Your spirit must serve as a General and Director over your soul and body.

You have the ability to do anything in this world. Your Spirit is what gives you inspiration to start a business, dream of doing something great and creating the life you want to live. But you must know your enemies. Your enemies are in you. Your emotions and inability to process yesterday, stops you from maximizing today. The choices you make with food, work habits, and the non-desire to exercise causes your body to be dysfunctional and therefore causes your soul and your body to war against your spirit. Your soul and your body are the appointed assassins in your life. They will lead a life of submission or they will ultimately be responsible for any and all personal frustrations, disappointments and griefs in your life. When the soul and body are in control, they seek to kill your spirit. All three [spirit, soul, body] are fighting to lead, but only one was designed to lead.

Law #7] A Spirit God will require Spirit-Filled Worship of its Deity

If your God is Spirit, than you must worship that God in spirit, through the life your inner-spirit is manifesting outward. If your god is a logical and emotional god, then you must worship anything that causes you to see life your way and without a shadow of a doubt you must live on an emotional roller coaster all the days of your life. If your God is Flesh, then your body must look its best at all times, rather it feels good or not, and you must sacrifice anything to look good to others. Decide now whom you will serve.

Law #8] The spirit of a person must be developed through the word of a Spirit God

Your God needs to talk to you and train you, how to grow and be strengthen through Him. The problem is, you are spirit, soul and body. So how can a spirit God talk to you, when appointed assassins are trying to block the enhancement of the spirit? The only way is through the written and spoken words of the Spirit God, without it, you are doomed to fail in the development of your spirit person.

Law #9] You must have a Spirit Guide

There must be someone assigned to you, to help you through the emotional episodes of life and the constant bombardment of ignorance that must be worked through for your spirit to develop. How do you connect to the Universe? What are your means of channeling energy beyond this world? Can you see the unseen? Find a spirit guide that can see what you don't see and forewarn you of the traps, dangers and bad environments of life. Find a spirit guide that will help you to overcome the weakness of the flesh and the limited abilities of your mind and heart.

Law#10] Your Spirit Guide must have three character traits.

1.] **Ability to teach**- which means your spirit guide, must understand your God better than anyone in the earth and be willing to teach you about your spirit God.
2] **Ability to comfort**- that means your spirit guide must be centralized to where you are and be ready to help you through anything.
3] **Ability to guide**- must be capable of empowering you to trust him; to lead you in the right way at all times.

Law#11] Always be conscious that you are connected to the Universe and know that the Universe is one with you.

Everything that is anything can be related to one thing or another. You are part of a master plan. You are the key that fits into a special door. That door no man can open but you. Wait for your time to start a chain reaction within the earth. Maybe it is a death of a loved one that will cause you to rise and do what you were intended to do. Maybe you will find the cure for cancer. Maybe you will find a way to stop world hunger. Do you doubt what is in your spirit? Why? It is that, which is in your spirit, that will propel your life to be full, enjoyable and with purpose.

Law#12] Command your vision to come forth

Stop waiting for someone to do what you know is inside of you to do. Stop waiting for the perfect day to begin. You must wake up in the morning and speak, plan, outline, and practice your vision daily. Oh, what a joy it will be to see you begin to speak your now into existence and live in each moment of its joy. The time is now for you to gird up your loins and find the inner-strength to prosper into your potential. No one is going to help you, until you help yourself. You attract into your life, what you believe about yourself. Start demanding the "better you" to show up and perform on the stage of life.

Law #13] Find a place of regeneration

Life has a way of overwhelming us. But, we have the ability to implement preventive measures before life overwhelms us with the voices of reason and chaos. Your God wants to talk to you alone from time to time. Find a place where you don't talk, but you listen. A place where everyone is not around you, but your God is speaking in you. Find the place at home or at work that is secluded for your moments of meditation with your God. The spirit person must be regenerated through its God. Stay conscious of the need to listen to your God. The benefits are priceless!

Law #14] Understand the difference between Purpose, Vision and Destiny

It is the essence of your spirit, the design of its creation and the heart of its creator. Your purpose, destiny and vision is locked up in your spirit and it must be recognized in order for you to proceed to the next level of happiness and success.

Purpose- is the reason behind everything that has happen in your life up until this point. It is the parents you were born to, the pain you have been allowed to experience and the understanding that you are designed perfectly to use your life experiences to elevate others. Outside of it all, your purpose daily is to elevate others rather it be to support or correct, the end result must always be to enhance, develop, inspire and encourage someone outside of our selves.

Vision- is the inner-sight, passion, and willingness to learn and grow into something that you love to do rather you get paid or not for doing it. Write your vision down for your future goals. Put a time table on achieving benchmarks within your vision. Challenge yourself to let go and separate things from you that are a threat to your vision. Furthermore in the end understand that your vision for living can only be comprehended when the foundation of your purpose is established within you. In adding together, see clearly that a working vision will propel you into your destiny.

Destiny- is a state of mind within an environment that confirms your Vision and celebrates your purpose for living. Destiny is the full-circle of your life. **Destiny is what you leave to the next generation.** It is your legacy. It unlocks the sight of the Universe. Martin Luther King Jr. and Gandhi died for all people to be treated fairly. Their Destiny was to die at the hands of their oppressors. Without their deaths, the world would be in worst off shape. Destiny is not about you; it is about the future lives of other people. Destiny shows you how you were always part of a bigger picture and a more perfect plan then you could have even imagined.

Law#15] Overcome the fear of death

Your spirit will not die. That is the real you. Death from this world has a way of being a very powerful enemy to your happiness and success. You see what happens is, we make the choice to live in anxiety and fear of tomorrow rather than enjoy the presence for the presence. The fear of death causes a person to fear living. You have missed out on enough! Go now! Live Now! Do it Now! Be able to say to yourself, "I did it"! You can't stop death, so why let death stop you from living? Lets Live and live good.

Law #16] Love is an action

Love is giving. Love understands. Love must be stronger than your selfish ambitions. The love of your God must be deep and beyond your human understanding. Love from your spirit, for your spirit knows how your God loves you. Give with kindness and give from the heart. Action love will fill your soul with contentment. Sharing love with family and friends will create a bond that serves as ointment to get through the wounds of life. Love someone today. Love them for being human. Love them for being alive. Love them for being in your life. Give the most precious gift in the universe to someone through your actions and not just your words. It is your gift, to give to someone else.

Law #17] The voice of reasoning is the enemy of your spirit

What causes internal frustration to reach the point of no return? What is the cause of diabolical depression and crippling self-esteem? It is the voice of reasoning. You have plans right "now" that are going unfulfilled. Save for, some plans are meant to be unfulfilled. So how do you separate the ones that are meant to be, from the ones that are not? You separate plans, goals, visions, purposes, and destinies by what you sense in your spirit that you are suppose to be doing. If your spirit is connected to a Spirit God, that Spirit God will speak into your spirit. The Spirit God will have your Spirit Guide confirm what your purpose is, and what your purpose is not. If you are connected to a Spirit God, He will show you the vision for your life and push you into your destiny. But, the enemy is always present to stop this powerful connection from manifesting in your life. The "voice of reasoning" is the enemy to your spirit and to a Spirit God. However, it is the friend of your soul and your body. If a Spirit God ever commands you to do something, it will be unequivocally always, "the voice of reasoning", that will attempt or succeed in stopping you from manifesting your best life today. The "yeah, but" crowd is the "voice of reasoning". The spirit of fear is the voice of reasoning. Culturally taught behavior is the voice of reasoning. Self-perception is the voice of reasoning. The lack of resources is the voice of reasoning. Past pain and unspeakable disappointments are the voices of reasoning. The spirit that is inside of you, has potential that you cannot even phantom. One man can change a nation, by believing what is in his spirit. One woman, can change the world, when she understands her purpose, vision and destiny. YOU are going to change your life today. You are going to trust your spirit to be your command center and you are going to bring your soul and body into submission of your authority. YOU are going to do it right now and forever!

THIS IS THE MEDITATION SECTION FOR NOTES, WRITE WHAT YOU FEEL AND WHAT YOU ARE THINKING RIGHT NOW ABOUT <u>YOU AND YOUR SPIRIT</u>

YOU have a soul.

[That which gives you consciousness,

emotions, the ability to reason,

to learn, to remember, to store information,

and to feel what other people feel.]

CHAPTER 5
Soul
19 Laws

Law #1] Find your self

Who are you? No not the person you portray, but really who are you. What are you not good at? Your weaknesses, your fears, How do you really feel about people of different races? What do you really want to say to your God, that you are afraid to say? Are you embarrassed of where you were raised? Do you hate your heritage? Society has created a standard that says, "If you tell the truth in public you will be punished". That I understand to some degree. But, if you fail to tell the truth to yourself about how you think and feel about issues, then you live a lie and a lie will kill your self-esteem.

Law #2] Have a management system in place to control your emotions

Emotions serve three purposes. They slow you down, speed you up or they cause you to stand still. Guilt, sadness and pain will slow you down. Excitement, anxiety and pleasure will speed you up. Jealousy, hate and unforgiveness will cause you to be unable to move forward. Count to 10 before you react! Or better yet know what frustrates you and know how to calm it done. Know when your emotions are speeding so much to the point that you fell to recognize the environment of the room. Understand when you are depressed; it is due to the fact that certain emotions are slowing you down. Last but not least, avoid allowing any emotion that is not healthy for you, to possess you and ensnare your precious time in the earth.

Law#3] You are what you see and what you hear

T.V, radio, CD's are training and developing your mind to see life the way it is portrayed through these mediums. Listen to angry music, you will live angry. Watch emotional movies, you will always be emotional. Do what you want to do, but know what you do; the media is helping you do. Control and understand the power of the media or be affected by its influence.

Law#4] Find a place of rest for your soul

Take a vacation please. Take a vacation every three months please. Turn off your cell-phone at least for one day a week please. The hustle and bustle of life can cause emotional overloads and the need to be refreshed from time to time is crucially important. Life is a grind, when you do the same things day in and day out. Regenerate your soul, take yesterday's problem and leaves it on your desk. Come back to it after your vacation and then take care of it.

Law#5] Do not trust your emotions to decide your future

Your emotions will destroy your potential. They love to cry I don't feel like it, I'm tired, I 'm mad at such and such and that is why I can't go to the business meeting. I don't like certain types of people and that is why I cannot live in that city. Oh your emotions have robbed you from maximizing your potential and have prevented you from getting where your suppose to be in life. Remember the enemy is in you.

Law#6] Confess your sins to God, not to man

Telling people your problems only creates chaos, gossip and misconstrued interpretations of your character. Why get mad at someone for telling your secret, that you told them? If it is something that can destroy your character, tell someone far away, whom you know you can trust. Learn to manage your affairs and the world won't be given the opportunity to laugh at you.

Law#7] Write it down

Write the plan for the day down. A lot of grief can be contributed to the lack of structure. Your day is your day. Write it down. Build systems of steps for your day. Bring order to your life. Without order the soul becomes wondrous. It begins to focus on things that rob you of your focus. There is nothing worse than living an unproductive day. If your plan is to rest for today, write it down. Understand that you must manage your soul or it will control you and eventually destroy you.

Law#8] Know your starting 5 [Parent, Teacher, Pastor, Community leader and Self] These are the major people that have influenced your life up until this point. They have assisted you, in how you have developed, into what you have used to identify your culture, community and belief in self. Be careful whom you submit your ears to. These are also some of the same people that will kill your spirit long-term. Did these starting five help you in life? Did one or all of them damage you in a way that is unthinkable to try to explain and heal from? Do you need to assess the things that they said or did to you 20 years ago? You could be living in success or failure right now based upon how your starting five has affected your life.

Law #9] Choose your friends, don't let them choose you

To many times we fail to interview people we call friends. Just because you have worked with someone for six months, does not make you friends with him or her. This by itself, a lot times causes unexpected heartache. Your friends are only people you have a clear understanding with. It is a relationship where a friend's role is understood and valued. Stop thinking because you meet someone at a club that now you are friends. Stop setting yourself up for failure.

Law #10] Laugh at yourself

It sure beats feeling guilty about something you did. So what; something didn't work out the way you wanted. Yeah, that was really stupid what you did. But, at the end of the day, there is always tomorrow. Find the humor in the situation and keep moving.

Law #11] Expectation causes Disappointment

If you expect too much from yourself, you are setting yourself up for disappointment. You are not going to get the project done within the time frame you have set. There are going to be road bumps in life. Anticipate, expect it! Traffic will be backed up, and you are going to have to learn how to manage it, even if you are running late.

Law #12] Yes it can happen to you

Get over yourself! What has happen to others can and will happen to you. Avoid the trap of thinking you are exempt from the perils of life. Two people can get fired from the same job and one goes on to start her own company, while the other becomes an alcoholic. Two people could lose a loved one, one goes on to start a non-profit organization; the other becomes bitter towards everyone that did not understand her pain. Life is going to throw you a fastball. A advise you to swing batter, batter swing. The shocks and awes of living can cause devastating psychological pain. Be ready, adapt, change, heal, grow, recreate, but never give in to the psychosomatic warfare of defeats, tragedies, shortcomings or failures.

Law #13] Cleanse your emotions of self-hatred

The subconscious part of you needs to surface and confess what it does not like about you. Put it all on the table! Your doubts, fears, and insecurities. The greatest mistake you can make is; believing that you have it all under control and to think that it is not affecting your life in a major way. It is affecting you! To not deal with the dark side of our self-perception opens the door for internal wounds to be filled with the bacteria of degenerate self-love. You have to self-love and the only way to get there and stay there is through dealing with your self-hatred.

Law #14] Forgive yourself with a purpose in mind and let go of the past

Forgiveness with purpose is the ability to have a complete and thoughtful approach to letting something go out of your life. Forgiveness with purpose understands that forgiving is more about you, than the person or situation you need to forgive. Forgiveness with purpose is glorification to a forgiving God. Forgiveness with purpose is the ability to block the thief of time from robbing your present joy. Forgive, but forgive with purpose and with a personal objective in mind that promotes and celebrates your spirit, soul and body. The past was designed to create lessons learned that are practiced and lived now. The past is not and should not be positioned within you to disintegrate your present joy. You are here today for a reason. I need your smile. I need your grace. But if the pass has locked in chains your today, how can you give me your best today? Ask yourself to live today. A successful day is happening right now. It is in each breath that you are breathing. Let go of the suffocation of yesterday. Breathe today! Breathe Now!

Law # 15] Let go of the need to judge

No one is perfect and no one will ever live up to your standard all the time. You will be let down by friends, family and enemies. Letting go of the need to judge others, frees up your energy to concentrate on understanding the lesson you can learn from a situation and how you can apply hard lessons to your future.

Law # 16] Sticks and Stones will break bones, but words will kill you

The words that are stored in your memory and the environment of people you subject yourself to daily are either elevating your self esteem or causing you to stay in a psychological trap within your mind and heart. Words are so powerful that once they enter the soul, they can dictate emotions and actions. Who are you allowing to enhance or infect your environment?

Law #17] Images, Pictures, and quotes create the environment of success

Take plenty of pictures along the way to your goal or destination. Create fun memories of your experiences. Put pictures and quotes up in your home and job that are positive and full of life. Create your environment through visuals that inspire you, quotes that stand the test of time and images that put a smile on your face.

Law #18] A good attitude comes out of balanced emotions

You can try to be positive and still be negative because you have not dealt with the emotional inconsistencies of your life. Positive people are generally happy people because they have balanced emotions. Not to high and not to low. Life is a journey, not a destination. Find the rhythm of your life and live in it today; that is what true positive attitudes are. Balance and harmony equals a great attitude!

Law #19] Change your Vocabulary

The words you speak are either building your self-esteem or tearing your-self worth down. Change the terminology that you use to describe your state of mind and your perception of reality. Let go of all foul language. Let it no longer be a part of your vernacular. Curse words and evil speaking of yourself and others, attracts negativity into your environment. Coin phrase terms that illuminate your heart, soul, mind and body. Challenge yourself to grab hold of words such as, "FANTASTIC", "GREAT", "AWESOME", I'M EXCITED", "EXCELLENT" "WHAT AN OPPORTUNTIY", "THANK YOU", AND "WOW". Allow your speech to uplift your mindset. Cleanse your memory of culturally taught speech and walk into your "now' with positive energy and beautiful expressions.

THIS IS THE MEDITATION SECTION FOR NOTES,
WRITE WHAT YOU FEEL AND WHAT YOU
ARE THINKING RIGHT NOW ABOUT
YOU AND YOUR SOUL

_____

_____

_____

_____

_____

_____

_____

_____

_____

_____

_____

_____

_____

_____

_____

_____

YOU are **body**, [*the physical image and reflection of what is going on in the spirit and soul of a person, the part of you that will rise to it greatest potential and just as fast begin to dissipate back to the earth from where it came*]

CHAPTER 6
BODY
15 LAWS

Law#1] The value of your body must be realized

How much of your destiny that you fulfill in the earth is directly tied to how you take care of your body. The inability to see your dreams prosper and visions come to pass, might be limited if health issues are a constant concern. Imagine, you personally can be the person that sets you back from living well because you have neglected your health. Could this be your time to make a difference in the world? Could you be the one that will raise the child that will bring balance to the earth? Are you healthy enough to see your purpose for living to the end? Then please, understand that your health is going to play a major role on how these questions are answered.

Law#2] Exercise does more for you than make you sweat

Use exercise to help you process stress, frustration and anger. Get on that treadmill and force all negative energy to leave your body. Did you know that exercise causes better oxygen flow in? When we inhale (breath in,) we are taking in oxygen. When we exhale (breath out,) we are letting out carbon dioxide, which the plants use to make more oxygen. Plants need the carbon dioxide, you need the oxygen. Create better breathing patterns through consistent exercising. Live a better day when you know, you did something in that day, to support a healthier lifestyle. See the big picture with exercising.

Law #3] Stretch your muscles to unify your body

Muscle stretching two to three times a day will calm the soul and keep the body fresh. When you take time out of the day to just stretch; you create harmony in the body and you free the soul to elevate itself from the days stress at hand. Stretch it out and stretch it often! Join a yoga class; Get a deep massage or just get somewhere by yourself for five minutes and just s-t-r-e-t-c-h.

Law#4] You are made of water

The adult human body is about 50 to 65 percent water according to the worldbank.
http://www.worldbank.org/depweb/english/modules/enviro

nm/water/, The body is not going to give you the extra push you need daily without it. Drinking plenty of water will also do wonders for your skin and help you to sleep better at night. Drink more water! Give the body what it needs to contribute to a successful day.

Law# 5] Find a family doctor

You are not a doctor and it is not going to get better in time. Nothing is more disturbing than knowing that some type of illness in your body could have been prevented, if you had used preventive measures. Your health is of great value. Your family wants you around down the road. There are no spare parts; so you only get one shot at taking care of this precious vessel. If your body is aching in anyplace, give it its' proper attention. Remember the message is preventive health care, not "repair- to-late" healthcare. If something does not feel right or if you have a headache, nasty cough or if something is not looking right to you, go see a doctor. This book is about happiness and success right? Then the success is keeping this temple balanced, healthy and in working order so that you can enjoy this moment in life. The happiness is living in the process of enjoying the ability to be responsible for the nurture and care of your body. Let's live strong and live good!

Law# 6] Take control of the times you eat

Eat every two to four hours. Always have something keeping your metabolism going. You use energy 24 hours a day. Keep the gas flowing with consistency of flow. Give your body an opportunity to process food in a relaxed state. It is when we eat large meals and have not eaten anything for 8 hours; that the body is tired and sluggish after a meal. If the body is being rushed with a lot of food all at once, it begins to pull energy from you to process that large meal and that will affect your emotions and mindset. Take control today!

Law #7] Eat in Moderation

If a pizza has 8 slices; eat 1 slice now and one slice later. Yes chocolate is good, but eat chocolate once a month. Food in itself is not bad for you. It is the over-indulging and lack of respect for what certain foods do to your body when done in excess, is what is bad for you. Eat to live, don't live to eat. Food cannot consume you anymore. Stop hiding behind it, it cannot save you from yourself. There is no reasoning in the body. You can eat cake and ice-cream everyday and the body will not tell you to stop. Your mind must be able to process when and what to eat and how much. You cannot eat till you are full. The decision must be made before you eat how much you are going to eat.

Law #8] Join others that want to improve in their body

Environment creates reality. In addition, the reality is, you probably do not want to work--out all the time. But, whom you surround yourself with is dictating your motivation to continue a work out plan, eating plan or how you view the importance of taking care of your body. Support groups are needed, especially where food and exercise is concerned. Too many people underestimate the seriousness of food addictions and obesity in the body. Don't be a shame to ask for help. I believe the only way, you can live your best now continually in your health, is to have a connected network of people, who are transparent and helpful in moments of weaknesses. Find people that inspire you to live healthy, because if the people around you now are not helping you, they are killing you slowly.

Law #9] Rest your body

If you are not getting the proper rest, happiness will never be real. The lack of rest will cause the body to effect the mind. Your rest must become a priority to you. One of the most powerful secrets to getting quality rest is to prepare yourself for sleep. You can prepare for rest by quieting the soul and body down at least an hour before you plan to physically sleep. Put the kids to bed, turn off the television and read something soft, kind and healthy for you. Why is your rest so important to your happiness and success? Because how you feel in the morning will dictate how you act throughout the day. Start the day with inner enthusiasm and focused energy!

Law # 10] Pray and ask your God to help you in maintaining your health

Surely your God cares about your body. He created it. He knows secrets about your specific body that maybe you have overlooked or have not considered. Pray for guidance in what you eat and when you eat it. Pray that God will deliver you from foods that are toxic to your system and foods that need to be eradicated from your lifestyle. Petition Him how to exercise and who to call on for assistance with your workout plan. Ask God to help; he is your friend, through thick and thin. Let him help to keep you healthy and full of life.

Law #11] Train the mind, don't let it train you

Understand that the body is always seeking confirmation from the mind. Let me explain. When the body is tired, it tells the mind that by sending feelings to the brain. Now the tipping point is rather or not the mind buys into the feeling or signal from the body. Your spirit will need to be strong first to train the mind not to confirm the body's tricks. You will only be tired when your mind believes it, not your body. Train your mind to obey your spirit. Don't let your body train your mind.

Law #12] Personal Hygiene plays a big part in being happy

Cleanliness reflects a level of acceptance on how you perceive life. You are responsible for cleaning your body, your home, and most of all your personal space. Sickness in the body can be caused from an unsanitized life-style. A dirty body and a dirty home can and will cause some form of depression. Take a shower, brush and floss your teeth, comb your hair, clean up that garage, clip those dirty fingernails, move the furniture around and do some spring-cleaning. Start the new you by cleaning up after the old you. It will make a big difference on your mood and attitude.

Law#13] Are you storing food or using food?

The paradigm shift must happen. Food is for fuel or energy to the body. Its purpose was never to be used as a storage material for the body. You get gas when you need it in your car, not when the tank is already full. Pay attention to how you see food. Why do you need to eat a large meal if you're going to bed in 2 hours? Food turns into fat if it is not used for energy. Paradigm shift your thinking and that alone will cause you to begin to understand food and how it correlates with your body.

Law# 14] Supplements are needed in today's society

Realize that the food we eat today does not have all the proper nutrients, vitamins, fiber or minerals that we need.

Part of potentially zapped energy is due to the lack of the body getting what it NEEDS from the food we eat. You may be depressed because of the lack of something in your diet. Call your doctor and get screened or get with a nutritionist and allow them to analyze your diet. It could be the difference between gaining or losing weight, smiling or crying, and depression or excitement. Get checked out! You have all to gain and nothing to lose.

Law #15] Food can become a drug to you

Food can become just as addictive as cocaine, marijuana and alcohol. Food can be used for entertainment just like cocaine, marijuana and alcohol. Food can become a silent killer just like......... Is Food your drug of choice? When a person is hooked on cocaine, they need professional help and so do you, if food is your drug to ease the pain and trauma in your life. It is unequivocally important to understand the delusional power of food as it attempts to medicate issues in your soul. You see when the soul is broken it will pull from the body to soothe it and when the body is broken, it will affect your self-esteem by constantly reinforcing to you, negative and degenerate thought processes that hinder, damage and imprison your self worth. Food can become an addictive drug to you. Don't let the drug called "food" make you an addict. "All drugs gain their potency through the wearing down of the mind" IJ

THIS IS THE MEDITATION SECTION FOR NOTES, WRITE WHAT YOU FEEL AND WHAT YOU ARE THINKING RIGHT NOW ABOUT <u>YOU AND YOUR BODY</u>

_____

_____

_____

_____

_____

_____

_____

_____

_____

_____

_____

_____

_____

_____

_____

_____

_____

Your ministry is much more than what you ideally perceive it to be. It is not just the preacher that preaches in a church or the missionary that travels overseas to feed the homeless. Your ministry is your purpose for being here. The vision that you see yourself being a part of and the destiny that was predestined before you where even born. WHAT ARE YOU HERE TO DO? What is the occupation, job or career that you are gifted, skilled at and love to do? You must fulfill your destiny. You must find what you are here to do.

CHAPTER 7
MINISTRY
18 LAWS

Law #1] What is your ministry? You are here to elevate others.

Rather it is through your job, community, church or business. Your career in the earth is designed to develop and train people to get to the next level in this life. Your life is not about you. It is about using your talents, skills and gifts to help others. The universe operates in a very dynamic motion. It simply says what you put out, will come back. If you want to be elevated from within, elevate someone outside of you. Teach a child that is blind. Train an employee that no one believes in. Smile at your neighbors. Take the back sit and support someone else's vision. Elevate! Elevate! Elevate!

Law #2] The law of help- you cannot help anyone who is not ready to be helped

No matter how good you are at doing your job or sharing your gifts with others; <u>please understand</u> that you can't help everybody. Let me go a step further. Not all people enjoy the work you do or how good you are at it. Get over it! You are not the savior of your company. People are entitled to believe what they want, from whom they want to believe it from. Wisdom says give to those that you know will appreciate it, not to those that will throw it back in your face.

Law #3] Go where you are needed, not just hired

Human nature will tell you that you are only appreciated where you are needed. No one, I mean no one wants to be in any occupation where they are disrespected or tolerated. Find the company, state, or person that needs what you can offer. This will breathe excitement in the workplace for you and reaffirm your purpose for being there. This is easier said than done. But, at the end of the day you will have to make a decision on rather you want to be happy long-term or miserable forever?

Law #4] Learn from someone you respect, not just someone you admire

I admire Evil Knieval but I do not respect a man who risks his life to entertain. Therefore I would never want to learn from him, how to jump 50 cars. The same principle applies in life. The people you respect are the one's you will find that can teach you how to do something better, in a field or subject that you want to know more about. You need a mentor, not a friend when it comes to your ministry. Your mentor will evoke uncomfortable emotions in you. But, in the end it always must be for <u>your good</u> not theirs.

Law # 5] Your ministry is a lifestyle, not a 9 to 5

Find a job that mirrors closely how you act, behave, and think rather you are at work or at home. You have been told the bad lie of, "leave your work at work and leave your personal business at home." What a bunch of crap! If something bad happens at work, it will affect you when you get home and vice versa. What you don't want to happen is to fall into a workplace culture that demands that you be fake the whole time you are there. Eventually you will explode. Find the company culture that fits your lifestyle. You will thank me later.

Law # 6] Learn to deal with people- there are four types of people you deal with everyday. People, who add, subtract, divide or multiply things in your life. Know where they fit into your mathematical equation. Let me explain.

PEOPLE+, -, /, x, PEOPLE+, -, /, x, PEOPLE

If they are **adding**, what are they adding? Stress, joy, pain, love, peace, confusion

If they are **subtracting**, what are they subtracting? Negative influences, the good people around you, low-self esteem, or trying to take your self-worth

If they are **dividing**, what are they dividing? Are they dividing right from wrong, good from bad, Are you being alienated from the group or separated from the group, for growth and development?

If they are **multiplying**, what are they multiplying? trouble in the office, your knowledge to do your job, how to spend money faster or save more money now.

PEOPLE+, -, /, x, PEOPLE+, -, /, x, PEOPLE

Learning to deal with people is crucial to your personal happiness. It is up to you to sort out the good, bad and the ugly. Don't kid yourself! The people in your life have a tremendous effect on you. Learn to manage the terrible boss or annoying co-worker. Learn to manage the sarcastic statements and obscene behavior. Don't let the bad stuff get in your soul or spirit. Manage it, be professional, but most of all be honest to yourself about the people around you.

Law #7] Understand what Self-definition means

If you allow someone outside of God and yourself to define you on what you are capable of doing and not doing, You will also be given that person the power to control how far you go within a chosen field. Stop allowing people to franchise their thoughts of your skill set. Better yet, stop buying into the limited thoughts of how you view yourself. See beyond your emotions. See beyond your comfort zone. Challenge is where you find out who you really are. Opposition is where true abilities are measured. Harness your skills. They are yours! They do not belong to the company you work for. You chose them, they did not choose you. You know your worth and what you bring to the table. Although you are not irreplaceable, you are good at what you do and you understand what challenges you are ready for and the ones that you are not ready for. Don't let the jealousy, discrimination, and envy of people that work with you, stop you from reaching for the stars. There are people waiting for you to come into position, so that they can see how wonderful of a place it is to work with you and for the company that you represent. Push hard, be consistent, be the best you can be, at all times!!

Law #8] Are you blessed or just lucky?

Anything that you recognize as being given to you by the Creator is a "blessing". Anything that you possess or can hold on to, that you recognize as being given to you by the Creator means you are "blessed". It signifies that the Creator choose you and gave to you, **to possess,** something that He or She felt was good for you to have at that time in your life. If you live by luck, then you are hoping in scientific numerical chances of possibilities to fall on whoever is randomly chosen at the moment. I like being blessed! If the creator choose me, then that means he considered 6.7 billion other people, but felt this was right for me to have. Luck does not create long-term relationships. Being blessed by your Creator allows you to celebrate your individuality and your personal relationship with your God. You are blessed my friend!!

WHAT ARE YOU HERE TO DO??
[THE 4 IF'S]

Law #9] If you are willing to do it for free....

If you have experienced the passion and joy you get from doing something you love and money cannot compare to the fulfillment you get from how it blesses other people. Then chances are either you have missed your calling or you need to quit your job and find a place to do what you love to do. If you don't, you will become bitter towards your family, friends and most of all yourself. Live the Dream! Live your Passion! This is not a dress rehearsal; you are on the stage of life.

Law #10] If you are willing to risk your life…

If you completely understand the danger of living your vision and fulfilling your ministry and still feel the need to do it, you have probably found the occupation that will lead you to your destiny. The threat of death usually is enough to detour people from things they thought they wanted to do. What are you willing to die for? What cause in the earth will make you sacrifice yourself for someone else's benefit? Don't let shame or fear stop you. It's your baby, your project, and your vision!

Law #11] If you are willing to let go of all your material belongings…

What a nice house you live in! And oh how you have been saving to buy that Mercedes Benz you have been dreaming of for years. Can you let it go? Is the call of your ministry more important to you than your outward appearance of success to society? Can you really let it go? If you can, you have probably found the occupation that will lead you into your destiny.

Law #12] If you are willing to let go of your family and friends…

You will be judged and called crazy. Perhaps even labeled unreasonable are better yet exiled from your family and friends. Is there anything worth doing that you would sacrifice your "comfort zone" and "support group" for? If there is, you have probably found the occupation, the calling, the ministry, the purpose for living, and the vision that is stronger than your life that will lead you into your destiny.

Conquer "the 4 ifs" and you will find your ministry

Law #13] There is no great reward, without great sacrifice

You are so special to the point that everything you perceive, as gain must be sacrificed in order for you to truly, truly be happy and successful. You must remove the mountain of stuff out of your way to see clearly. Happiness is given to those who understand the rules. What are you willing to sacrifice for your happiness and success? How bad do you want to be happy? There are things you must let go. Starting with people you know and things that have tied down your creativity and your will to live. Let it go! It will hurt for now, but it will bring new joy later. Let it go! Your future success depends on it.

Law #14] Stay ready and prepared for your BIG OPPORTUNITY

Practice your skills; Practice your gifts, Practice, Practice, and Practice. Opportunity is coming rather you are ready or not. If you are ready, it is because you have practiced when no one was looking, you have been educated on your career opportunities that are coming your way and you have learned crucial skills that will be needed to be successful within your ministry, job or career.

Law #15] Do not despise small beginnings

Humble yourself, Learn what to do and not to do wherever you are at. Appreciate and except every moment and opportunity you are granted to be a part of an organization that is doing something that you love to do, Even if they are not doing it the way you want it done. You are there to learn from those around you. Inhale every breath of the environment. Don't get ahead of yourself. Stay humble and live in the moment. Elevation will come.

Law #16] Geographic repositioning is necessary

How would it feel to be talented enough for a job, but not mature enough for a position? The inability to deal with certain types of people can be a trap for failure. Get exposed to different cultures as fast as possible. People miss their calling everyday because certain types of people are intolerable to them. So they end up working a "comfort job" instead of a "life-fulfilling job". Travel and get exposed. Learn and grow. Mature and develop. You will thank me later.

Law #17] Don't try to solve EVERY problem at your job or you will become the problem

You can't carry the weight of the world. Neither are you the savior of everything that goes wrong at work. Use wisdom. Choose what problems will receive your attention and decide before hand, how far you will go to solve the problem. It is a trap to get you mentally stressed out at work. When you come home mentally beat down from work, you have nothing left to give to anyone else. People will use you up and spit you out, IF YOU LET THEM. Manage your day, manage your time, be wise, be strong, but know when to let go.

Law #18] Dress for Success

Dress to make yourself feel empowered, confident and assured. Never dress to just look good. It is much bigger than someone else looking at you. It is you giving off positive and focused energy in the work environment. Clothes carry energy. Good and Bad energy. Seductive and Professional Energy can be felt from clothing. What you wear does effect your emotions and your attitude. Successful clothing must be comfortable, not tight. Happy clothing must be clean and pressed, not dirty and wrinkled. Change some part of clothing while at work at least once a day. Why?@#? Stay fresh, feel fresh, every moment is an opportunity to give you and the world your best you. Allow the energy of fresh, clean, lively clothing to facilitate your best you.

THIS IS THE MEDITATION SECTION FOR NOTES,
WRITE WHAT YOU FEEL AND WHAT YOU
ARE THINKING RIGHT NOW ABOUT
**YOU AND YOUR MINISTRY
[JOB, CAREER OR OCCUPATION]**

_____

_____

_____

_____

_____

_____

_____

_____

_____

_____

_____

_____

_____

_____

_____

_____

_____

Your marriage is not just saying; "I do" to someone you love. But, it is at its root, the covenant or promises you have made to yourself. It is the moral code of being responsible and accountable. The promise to love, forgive and understand yourself first and the willingness to keep it real with the person you look at in the mirror daily.

CHAPTER 8
MARRIAGE
16 LAWS

Law#1] Love and Care for Your Self first, before you attempt to love and care for someone else

Take yourself to the movies before you ask someone out on a date. How you treat you, will determine how you will treat me. Don't ask me to take care of myself, if you fail to take care of yourself. If you have never had to love yourself through trying times, then how can you be supportive to someone else? It does not work that way. You will treat others that you bring into your life, the same way you treat yourself when no one is looking, I guarantee it. It is a terrible thing to have a successful wedding, but a failed marriage! Your ability to manage your body, soul, spirit, ministry, marriage and money now before you get married and have children is a direct reflection of how you will manage your spouse and children in the future. This book becomes absolutely necessary if you plan to get married or have children. You can't give someone else something that you don't have to give to yourself. Generational behavior that cripple's families for 300 years can be contributed back to men and women who failed to love self first before they started a family. If you are already married, then become an even better spouse with these tools. If you are a parent, then become a better parent with these tools. Get better, live better, be good, and live great!

Law#2] Know what your personal moral code is, you live by

What you like, you make excuses for and what you dislike, you judge. Your morals are based upon what you like and dislike. Some people feel that it is morally wrong to drink, smoke, or gain weight. How do you feel about it? Don't invite someone into your life and you're not clear about what upsets you and what you make excuses for. Stop being wishy-washy. Stand where you stand and let people know where you stand on issues in life. At the end of the day, another person must be given the chance to like you for you, not for who they think you are.

Law#3] Sometimes you can be right and still be wrong

The strong must bear the weaknesses of others in covenant relationships. If you judge others who you need, you lack the understanding to deal with them and soon it will cause the relationship to end. Understand the people around you and you will not have the desire to prove that you are right all the time. You see if you need me and you are always trying to prove your point, then eventually I will leave you and resent you, and then you will be without what you need. Self-preservation a lot of times comes at the willingness to give a little and take a little. The world does not revolve around your opinion. This must get down in your innermost being or you will miss your time to be good, fruitful and loving.

Law#4] The promises you make, reveal your character when they are tested

Character is the consistency of a person's behavior over time. Do you make consistent, empty promises to yourself? How do you react under pressure? You need to know the difference between what you say you're going to do and what you actually do. Character breed's reputation, reputation gives you a label or name. The name that you are identified with creates the foundation and values for any relationship to last and be healthy. You need to measure the character of you, not me, you. Love you, need you, laugh at you. Build your own character from within that brings stability to your life. That is strength and areas of improvement that money cannot buy.

Law#5] Talk to yourself or write down how you feel about real challenges in your life [THIS TRANSLATES TO HOW YOU WILL COMMUNICATE IN MARRIAGE]

You are not crazy if you talk to yourself. Who else can you trust more than you? Communicating your feelings in verbal or written form will filter out the confusion that emotional overloads will bring. Don't let life pile up on you. Find the release. It is for you and only you. Turn on the faucet of expression rather it is good or bad. Get it out. Humble yourself and speak your fears and doubts out. Don't let life become an overflowing river of weight. Challenge yourself today to set aside the weight that life can bring from time to time. Why is this principle so crucial? When or if you get married to someone, there is such a thing known as the "place of no return". Communication breakdowns in relationship are a lot of times, due to no one talking, until it is too late and too painful. Learn to talk about issues before they become "marriage-life threatening" to your relationship with your spouse.

Law# 6] Find the time to celebrate others

Someone will praise you, if you praise others. Divert from self-indulgence and find a way to congratulate, inspire and motivate others. It will cause you to be connected to the world and re-cur favor back on your own life. There are people around you right now that are beautiful and glorious. Get excited about someone else's achievements and passions. Support your spouse and go to your kids dance recital. Live in the moment of benefiting others. The universe has created those moments just for you to be a part of someone else's happiness.

Law# 7] Never make a career decision behind someone you are dating

Resentment will kill your dreams, when you allow temporary soul-ties to disrupt your destiny. Covenants that have consequences for both parties are the only times you should make the decisions that incorporate how it will affect someone else's life. All relationships are not permanent. Some are temporary, very temporary! Be able to walk away from what you know, you do not want long-term. Avoid the grievous error of putting 'fun before focus' and a 'good time before a good life.'

Law #8] Get mad and then get over it

Anger is a supernatural emotion that moves at the speed of light. Slow anger down. Holding on, to the emotion of anger can cause your downfall. Learn how to get mad slowly, but process that anger quickly. Anger can rob you of your daily moments of goodness and joy. But, it is real and it must be processed and abandoned or it can become reckless to yourself and others. Your time on the earth is short. Anger will rob you of precious moments of compassion, forgiveness and love. If you love me, give me your best you, all the time. That is what a healthy relationship needs.

Law # 9] Be careful whom you let into your personal life

Your personal life is where you open your heart to others. It is a place of emotional attachment, intimacy and most of all, "vulnerability". Put every relationship you have in its perspective. Learn to interview people just as if they were applying for a job. Yes, it is that important. One bad seed can cost you the next 10 years of your life. One new co-worker, who starts hanging out with you, can get you fired from a job that you have been doing great at for 20 years. Your heart is not to be shared with everyone. Learn to love people from a distance when needed. Be careful how you allow relationships to mingle.

Law# 10] "Just because you are making a good living, it does not mean you are living good"

Get over it! Money ALONE cannot buy happiness or success. There are people in your life that love you that you have not spent quality time with. Learn now or Regret later. Family is first, health is priority and your job was created to support the values you have in your life. Living for the dollar is a lie. Working 15-hour days, six days a week, is a lie. Stop living the lie, and start living in the balance your body, soul, spirit, and marriage deserve.

Law # 11] You have a right to good sex

Some people say that sex is overrated. But sex has caused more relationships, covenants, promises, and codes of conduct to be violated in marriage than probably anything else. Stop having sex with people if you don't understand what you need in your sex life. You are only creating misery for yourself and your partner. Sex is a big part of your happiness and it must be respected and communicated to your partner in order for it to be successful to you and them.

Law# 12] Prepare children for life, not to be your drug for you not living life

If you give your children everything they want now, they will be dysfunctional adults in life. They will want all relationships to mirror the lifestyle they lived at home with their parents and guess what? In the end your heart will be broken from your offspring's inability to adjust to real life. So either train now for life, or pay for it later. Soon your resources and influence to do something about it will be limited, especially when they grow up.

Law#13] Why have children, if you can't afford them?

Children cost money and they deserve the best you

have to offer. Is it the child's fault, when you must sacrifice your lifestyle to take care of them? Why harbor anger and frustration towards children? Did they ask to be born into this world? Have you had the opportunity to be adventurous and do all the things you want to do? Why set yourself up for internal failure and mixed emotions? Children are a blessing, but they are only a blessing to you when the time is right. Don't rush to have children because your neighbors have four children. Enjoy your life! This is your time! A child is a lifetime investment. Are you ready to be responsible for someone else outside of yourself? If you are not, chill! Relax and enjoy yourself! Enjoy the world while it is yours to enjoy, because when children are brought into the world they are your world.

Law#14] Who married who? Did you marry the person or did the person marry your family?

Marriage is about you and the person you are married to. Please don't get married if your mother, father, sister, brother, best friend is more important to you than your spouse. It is a complete disaster and it will cause your spouse to leave you eventually. Unnecessary heartache over immature behavior is conquered by the wisdom to know what to do and what not to do. Marriage is probably the most serious thing you will ever do. Don't destroy what you have, even before it is given a chance to grow. Keep your family out of your business, because it is imperative that you do so.

Law#15] The person you're married to will change

The person you married will change with the seasons of life. They will morph into a greater or lesser self than what you married. Be ready for the change. Change with the change. Different career paths change people. Promotions on jobs change people. Children change people. Death changes people. But the challenge is, you are married to the person that is changing right before your eyes. Welcome to the seasons of life. The trees in the earth must adapt to all four seasons if they wish to survive and so must you, if you hope for your marriage to stay strong. Maybe your spouse does not want to stay home anymore and watch the kids, maybe he or she wants to start a business and let you watch the kids?@#. Will you be ready for the change in yourself or the person you have committed your life to? Your happiness will rely on your ability to adapt and move forward. If you can't, your marriage is good as dead!

Law #16] Empower your spouse

Speak positive words of encouragement to your spouse. Support visions and goals that your significant other has. Talk to your spouse about things that you know are important to them. Love them first and often before you seek to correct them. Do at least one thing a week that surprises them and that shows them, that you are thinking of them. If you are not married, do all these things for yourself or for a close family member or friend. Cherish the moments to build up your spouse.

THIS IS THE MEDITATION SECTION FOR NOTES, WRITE WHAT YOU FEEL AND WHAT YOU ARE THINKING RIGHT NOW ABOUT
YOU AND YOUR MARRIAGE [MARRIAGE IS ABOUT CHARACTER, PROMISES, SELF-COMMITMENT]

_____

_____

_____

_____

_____

_____

_____

_____

_____

_____

_____

_____

_____

_____

_____

_____

Your money tells the story of your ability to manage the one thing that is a threat to your relationship with God. It tells the chronicle of a busted character trait, undeveloped business mind, unmanageable life style and the need to justify your existence. It also is your legacy in which your offspring will be measured with to rather you did what was right with the money you had while you lived in the earth.

CHAPTER 9
MONEY
15 LAWS

Law #1] Knowledge and Understanding of money is better than having money itself

A fool can have money, but only a wise person can keep money generating in his or her life. Start learning today what a bank really does and what is interest, credit score, FICO score, creditors, debt, income, assets, liabilities, income statements, balance sheets, investors, bills and expenses are before you focus to much time on just getting more money. There is no greater failure in finances then to have had money and lost it. Know what money is and understand how it works. A fool can make money, but only the wise can keep it. You can find money on the street, but if you lack money management skills, you will lose that which you have in your hand. Take classes on money management skills. You won't regret it. If you take care of your money, your money will take care of you.

Law #2] Money is generated through your mind and heart

Money itself is not real. Your talents, skills and gifts generate your money every day for you. Please find what you are good at. If you do; the money will follow. If you search within yourself, there is a mountain of gold inside of you. Get that shovel and dig it out. You are not designed to chase money. Money is designed to chase individuals and be released to those that use their talents, skills and gifts to make money. If it is the wrong job; quit and quit today! So much bitterness of life is generated through doing jobs that do not fit who you are. Don't live in bitterness because of the lack of self-consciousness of how money flows. Your money is in you! Pull it out of you and let the world see how wonderful you are.

Law #3] Money is the god of things

Money is a god, which many people worship in order for money to give them things. Is money your God? Do you sacrifice your health, emotional state, family, friends, and self for it? Are you willing to lie, steal, cheat and murder for it? If so, money is your god. Every god wants to be served faithfully and held in honor at all times above all things. Money wants to be your god while you are living in the earth. It is a choice and the question of temptation that must be truly answered without prejudice. Is money your god?

CAUTION: YOU CAN ONLY ANSWER THE QUESTION IF YOU ARE READY TO TELL YOURSELF THE TRUTH.

Law #4] Money cannot be your God if you want true happiness and success

> Q: When is money your God?
> **A: <u>When you try to get your money to do a thing that only your God can do, that's when you know that money is your god</u>**

What can money not do for you?

Money cannot……

Prevent diseases, change painful memories, heal your soul, give you life, make someone love you or make you love someone, make you love yourself, deliver you from anger, give you wisdom or understanding, give you a healthy self esteem, stop you from cheating on your spouse because your lust is out of control, stop you from doing drugs and alcohol, stop you from lying, it cannot stop death from coming, give you peace, joy and contentment, money cannot replace time, money cannot give you talents or gifts, money cannot heal a broken heart, money cannot restore a marriage, give you favor with God, it cannot buy your way into heaven, wake you up in the morning, cure cancer, AIDS or herpes, make you a better person, save you from yourself, or buy love.

Money can buy a house, but it cannot buy a home
Money can buy a family van, but not a family
It cannot buy character, integrity or morals
Money cannot buy good health
Money cannot buy the Holy Spirit
Money cannot give you the blood of A Saviour that washes away all your sins or give you peace with God and yourself

WHAT ARE YOU TRYING TO GET MONEY TO DO THAT ONLY GOD CAN DO? WHAT ROLE DOES GOD NEED TO PLAY IN YOUR LIFE THAT MONEY CAN'T?

_____

Law # 5] If you want money, get around people who know and understand how money works

Environment, Environment, Environment will and always will dictate how you respond to money, life and problems. Exposure to people with money, will teach you how they think, move and act. Poor people re-confirm their environments by staying around other people that are just as poor as they are. Climb out of the hole! Allow your ignorance of money to be put in the presence of money thinking people. If Bill Gates is on television; stop what you're doing and listen to every single word he says. Something will jump out at you, if you humble yourself, and get around the right people, that can help you get to the next level in your finances.

Law # 6] Understand the difference between getting rich, having prosperity and being wealthy and living poor [learning this LAW will give you the big picture]

You will live in one, the other or all four. So understand what it means to get rich, have prosperity, and be wealthy or live poor.

Getting rich- is about having more than needed or having a surplus of money. Usually it happens within a certain time frame of being in the right place at the right time. Yep! Getting rich is based on playing the odds and getting in the game of chance. You don't have to be smart to be rich, but you do have to be willing to take chances and be willing to take major risk.

Having prosperity- is about constant growth and development with money. Prosperity is usually reserved for the conservatively but, savvy investor who thinks long-term about money and believes that future money is better than present money.

Being wealthy-is about being able to generate money through other people. This is the lead-thinker when it comes to money. The person who gets money through wealth understands team, positions and roles that must be played. Wealth will sustain a family legacy. Wealth is a mindset of how to effectively deal with people. Yes, the Rockefellers are rich, but they are wealthy because of how they are able to influence the lives of people that work within many of their companies. You need to know this, so that you can focus on how money plays a role in your life.

Living Poor- is about a hand to mouth mentality. It is the person that goes out and works for a check himself or herself and tries to get money by themselves. Only the poor think that way. Some parents to this day believe that "hard work will get you ahead". I understand now that it is the lie spoken by people who have a "live poor" mentality. The Rich tell their children, "take a chance, and be strong". The Prosperous tell their children, "Be smart, make wise investments, "take care of your money and your money will take care of you". The wealthy tell their children, "Treat people with respect, and understand the value of relationships, partnerships, and covenants". "Take care of the people that take care of you". While those that live poor tell their children, "work hard" prove your loyalty by working harder than anyone else at that job" "Don't worry about tomorrow, just work hard today".

\\

How do you want to live your financial life? Do you like being poor? Do you really want to be rich? Is that important to the quality of your life? Do you want to be comfortable and not have to worry about the future? Do you want to create a residual strategy of creating and having money in your life?

YOU have got to figure this out for yourself. But for your own sanity, put money and the pursuit if it in its place. The ideal place will be a place that fits your lifestyle, not the ambitions of society, your family or your background.

Law# 7] Control your money by controlling your emotions

All out of control spending is directly tied to emotions. Remember the three purposes of your emotions? They slow you down, speed you up or cause you to stand still. Guilt, sadness and pain will slow you down; so you go shopping to make yourself feel better. Excitement, anxiety and pleasure will speed you up, so you spend freely not caring about tomorrow. Jealousy, hate and unforgiveness will cause you to be unable to move, and then you stop giving to help others and therefore you stop the universe from blessing you with more money. Learn to deal with your emotions. It is affecting your money!

Law #8] Your credit report is your greatest resource to get resources

You need dependable transportation. You need money for emergencies. But if your credit is jacked up, life will become almost unbearable. You will lack the ability to move freely and will be burdened with everything second hand and the need for others to help you. Take care of your credit. Better yet, learn how to, take care of your credit. It is embarrassing and humiliating when every bank in the world knows you have poor money management skills. Credit has become a key component of societal rankings. If you can't be trusted to take care of your money and pay your bills, the world will alienate it self from you. Failure to heed to this law, will cause you pain that will take years to recover from.

Law #9] Implement the "three collective practices" in your business life to create an environment of wealth and prosperity

1] *Find, train and develop the right team of people that, **directly work with you**, who appreciate and respect your leadership*
2] *Subcontract out work to individuals that excel in a particular discipline focus that helps you to maximize your day, your time and your business.*
3] *Partnership with others in investing capital or other tangible assets, to contribute to a business idea or concept.*

The wisdom to know how to create wealth and grow in your finances can be yours if you stay conscious of the three collective practices. You are not a genius in every thing that you do and without the words "team" "partnerships" and "group-thinking", I can promise you, that no one will support your wealth ambitions long-term. Bank of America is not, one of the largest banks without its people, partnerships and open ears to hear what is working and what is not. The right work environment will always determine how far and how fast you rise in your income. Surround yourself with people who are smarter than you. Real wealth, takes real money. If others have something to lose, they will invest their knowledge and understanding to help the business be profitable. Be honest, and know what your good at and what someone else is better at. "A half of a watermelon is better than having a whole pea". The collective practices will bring energy, challenges and intensity to your wealth and prosperity. Become uncomfortable to live comfortable.

Law #10] Talk to your money

Budget your checkbook. Come up with a yearly budget. Track your expenses. Watch where you spend most of your money! Then ask yourself why you buy what you buy. You must develop a real, romantic, working relationship with money in order for your money to respond to you when you need it. If money is abused, ignored, or not respected, it will embarrass you and leave you deceased when you need it the most. Do you live on a budget? Are you paying attention to that budget? If you only planned to spend $50 dollars on grocery and you spent $350 that might indicate to you a problem. If you pretend that you don't see the obvious then the obvious will become painful and embarrassing. Would you like to buy a 2008 BMW 740i? Do you have $90,000 cash lying around or can you afford a $1900 dollar a month car payment. Listen to your money; it will save you down the road if you respect the truth of where you are at financially. Keeping up with Joneses, Smiths and Jackson's are never realistic or practical money practices for you. Let's try keeping up with what's real with our own money and lifestyle and be content with it first. Learn now or learn later!

Law # 11] Never lend money to friends, if you hope to get it back

Friendships can and will be destroyed by money. Don't let your friends lie to you about borrowing money. Set the stage, before the relationship is betrayed. Only give money to friends never let them borrow. If you don't have $5000 to give, then give them $500 towards the goal of what they wanted to borrow. Money has a funny way of bringing out deceptive and evil behaviors from people we love. Don't let money suffocate your willingness and freedom to love friends and family.

Law#12] Important business relationships are more important than money

Learn the value of the gift a person brings into your life. Money will come and go, but a man or woman with integrity, character, accountability and responsibility is priceless. Once you know a person that you are doing business with, learn to manage the relationship and the money will take care of itself. In addition, make it your business to learn other people's strengths and weaknesses that you work with and learn how to move within the strengths and weaknesses of others by knowing your own. Life is not perfect, but you sure can have some fun with it, if you know how to dance on the stage of life.

Law #13] Rainy days are coming, always have an umbrella

Pay yourself first! Life is full of surprises and money can protect you from a lot of those surprises. Murphy's Law lets me know that the worst is going to happen at some point in your life. The sad part is not being financially ready when it does. Being fired from a job is a whole lot more fun when your bills are paid up six months in advance. Learn that you control your life style and if you control it, then manage it. Why give a job the ability to affect your joy if you lost the job? Let it rain, Let it rain, Let it rain, just don't get wet, you might catch a cold and that could be hard to recover from.

Law #14] Pay your bills

Character is built through accountability and responsibility. When you run from obligations that you know 100% that you are responsible and accountable for, you create darkness for your personal self worth. Pay your bills and hold yourself accountable for the image you project to yourself. Not paying your bills will trouble your mind and cause emotional instability. Take care of yourself and pay your bills the best you can.

Law #15] Be a giver

Money can be used to feed the homeless, build water systems in foreign countries, support runaway kids from the streets. Don't you want to be a part of that? The world is your community. You live in this community. One dollar could feed a starving family in a third world country. Give of your surplus, share with the world how fortunate you are and how much you appreciate the opportunity to give to others. Give it away for free and it will come back to you in ways that you can't imagine. Free is not just free. Free is empowering. Free is Future Residual Economic Empowerment [F.R.E.E.]. The world is waiting on you to be a giver. Find a box today and put some nice goodies in there to help someone less fortunate than you. You are a good person and the world community needs you.

[AUDIO-CD ENDS HERE]

THIS IS THE MEDITATION SECTION FOR NOTES, WRITE WHAT YOU FEEL AND WHAT YOU ARE THINKING RIGHT NOW ABOUT
YOU AND YOUR MONEY

_____

_____

_____

_____

_____

_____

_____

_____

_____

_____

_____

_____

_____

_____

_____

_____

_____

_____

_____

CHAPTER 10
Are YOU qualified to change?

Are you waiting on the world to change before you change? If the world changed, would it change you? Are YOU qualified for change? Change is only prepared for **three types** of people. Either it is for people, that possess the defeat, pain, and anguish of not changing or reserved for individuals that have the mindset to get even better than what they are now or both. If the **pain** of not changing is **lesser** than the **need** to change, you will not take the necessary action needed to improve your life. If you are not the type of person to seek personal development in your life, it simply means you are comfortable and truly are terrified with change. Pain or the perception of pain, discomfort or fear must be **substantially greater** than just the **need** to change for anyone, I mean for anyone to really see the need to change. Why desire to change if you have maximized your potential in life? Why want change if your body is in perfect shape? Why covet change if nothing has ever caused you unimaginable pain? Why change if you don't need a God? Why consider change if your marriage is picture perfect? Why change if you have no debt and you have your financial life under control?

If change is for you, then you must practice the changes you want to make. Change is not automatic. Change is a revolution. It is not a switch to be clicked on or off, at any given moment. Change requires the ability to focus on a new or higher level of reality. Change requires the desire to want it bad enough, to be willing. Change requires practice.

In order to get to the **Third level of consciousness, you must practice the Laws or principles that will govern your own happiness and success.** Change requires that you start the process of change. The ideal of the 100 laws is that you migrate from oblivious thinking concepts to conscious principles that can be measured, taught and infused into your everyday life. *Remember, those who have mastered the art of the systems of life and codes of self-elevation only continually experience perpetual happiness and genuine success. Happiness and Success are learned behaviors and if they are learned, than you can learn how to be happy and* *successful*. Mastery of an idea is a journey of doing what is best, when you can remember the discomfort of doing what was unsuccessful. Practice the journey of your contentment. Take the active motions of self-initiation and move forward into your "now". Carry out the plan and fulfill the mission to live and live good. Live out of the abundance of a balanced lifestyle. Change from doing what has been unsuccessful and unfulfilling and practice the 100 laws of happiness and success. The time is now!

Next, there is a five-day plan/Third level of Consciousness exercise to help you begin the process of living to your fullest potential. Find 12 laws to practice a day, over a five day period and document what you felt throughout the day on the third level practice sheets. The third level practice sheets are located on the upcoming pages. To add to the structure of the exercise, select two laws a piece within the six Responsibilities Of Living Life [R.O.L.L.] [Spirit,Soul,Body,Ministry,Marriage,Money] to practice daily. In the practice sheet you will notice an area for "What 12 laws will you practice today?" There you will position the law number of two laws that you have chosen to practice and the page numbers on where the laws are located and how they can serve as a quick reference to turn to that page in the book, to reflect on the dialogue that was shared about the nature of that law. Underneath that, you will find the statement, "What does it say" so that you can have a quick reference of what the actually title of the law says. **For the first two days**, I have selected 24 laws for you to practice and document. After you have completed the first two days, you will have to choose for yourself, which 12 laws a day you want to practice **for the last three days.**

Practice the change you want to live. Change requires practice, and practice must be tangible and real. Use the wisdom, structure, and tools of this experience to penetrate all things that have worked against you, being united with YOU. Successfully complete the challenge and then receive the reward for challenging yourself. That alone is the success, "just challenge yourself "and that alone will be success all by itself.

THIRD LEVEL PRACTICE SHEET [DAY 1]

5-DAY PLAN/THIRD LEVEL CONSCIOUSNESS

tODAY'S DATE	SPIRIT	SOUL	BODY	MINISTRY	MARRIAGE	MONEY
[DAY 1] WHAT 12 LAWS WILL YOU PRACTICE TODAY?	LAW #1 AND LAW #14	LAW #5 AND LAW #16	LAW #2 AND LAW #6	LAW #9 AND LAW #14	LAW #3 AND LAW #12	LAW #8 AND LAW #13
WHAT DOES IT SAY?	LAW #1 FIND YOUR GOD [pg 15]	Law #5 Do not trust your emotions to decide your future [pg31]	Law #2 Exercise does more for you than make you sweat [pg42]	Law #9 "If you are willing to do it for free... [pg58]	Law #3 "Sometimes you can be right and still be wrong [pg68]	Law #8 "Your credit report is your greatest resources to get resources [pg 88]
WHAT DOES IT SAY?	LAW #14 Understand the difference between Purpose, Vision and Destiny [pg22]	Law #16 Sticks and Stones will break bones, but words will kill you [pg36]	Law #6 take control of the times you eat [pg44]	Law #14 "Stay ready and prepared for your Big Opportunity [pg60]	Law #12 "Prepare children for life, not to be your drug for you not living life [pg73]	Law #13 "Rainy days are coming, all ways have an umbrella [pg92]

Write Down what you are feeling and thinking throughout the day here?

_____
_____
_____
_____
_____
_____

What are you learning about yourself?

_____
_____
_____
_____
_____
_____

THIRD LEVEL PRACTICE SHEET [DAY2]

5-DAY PLAN/THIRD LEVEL CONSCIOUSNESS

TODAY'S DATE	SPIRIT	SOUL	BODY	MINISTRY	MARRIAGE	MONEY
[DAY 2] WHAT 12 LAWS WILL YOU PRACTICE TODAY?	LAW #2 AND LAW #15	LAW #4 AND LAW #15	LAW #3 AND LAW #7	LAW #8 AND LAW ##15	LAW #2 AND LAW #13	LAW #7 AND LAW #14
WHAT DOES IT SAY?	LAW #2 Make up your mind which God yo will serve[the God that is or the God that you want to be God [pg16]	Law #4 Find a place of rest for your soul [pg17]	Law #3 Stretch your muscles to unify your body [pg42]	Law #8 Are you blessed or just lucky? [pg57]	Law#2 Know what your personal moral code is, you live by [pg68]	Law #7 Control your money by controlling your emotions [pg88]
WHAT DOES IT SAY?	Law #15 Overcome the fear of death [pg23]	Law #15 Let go of the need to judge [pg35]	Law #7 Eat in Moderation [pg44]	Law #15 Do not despise small beginnings [pg61]	Law #13 Why have children, if you can't afford them?[pg73]	Law#14 Be a giver [pg92]

Write Down what you are feeling and thinking throughout the day here?

_____
_____
_____
_____
_____
_____

What are you learning about yourself?

_____
_____
_____
_____
_____
_____

THIRD LEVEL PRACTICE SHEET [DAY3]

	5-DAY PLAN/THIRD LEVEL CONSCIOUSNESS						
TODAY'S DATE	SPIRIT	SOUL	BODY	MINISTRY	MARRIAGE	MONEY
[DAY 3] WHAT 12 LAWS WILL YOU PRACTICE TODAY?						
WHAT DOES IT SAY?						
WHAT DOES IT SAY?						

Write Down what you are feeling and thinking throughout the day here?

_____
_____
_____
_____
_____
_____

What are you learning about yourself?

_____

_____

_____

_____

_____

_____

THIRD LEVEL PRACTICE SHEET [DAY4]

5-DAY PLAN/THIRD LEVEL CONSCIOUSNESS							
TODAY'S DATE	SPIRIT	SOUL	BODY	MINISTRY	MARRIAGE	MONEY
[DAY 4] WHAT 12 LAWS WILL YOU PRACTICE TODAY?						
WHAT DOES IT SAY?						
WHAT DOES IT SAY?						

Write Down what you are feeling and thinking throughout the day here?

_____
_____
_____
_____
_____
_____

What are you learning about yourself?

_____
_____
_____
_____
_____
_____

THIRD LEVEL PRACTICE SHEET [DAY5]

5-DAY PLAN/THIRD LEVEL CONSCIOUSNESS							
TODAY'S DATE	SPIRIT	SOUL	BODY	MINISTRY	MARRIAGE	MONEY
[DAY 5] WHAT 12 LAWS WILL YOU PRACTICE TODAY?						
WHAT DOES IT SAY?						
WHAT DOES IT SAY?						

Write Down what you are feeling and thinking throughout the day here?

_____
_____
_____
_____
_____
_____

What are you learning about yourself?

_____

_____

_____

_____

_____

_____

CHAPTER 11
DO YOU have the audacity to live happy and be successful? WHO DO YOU THINK YOU ARE?

You are what you live. You cannot fake what you are to yourself. The <u>consistency of your behavior</u> is the only thing that can measure how you live. Living requires that you accept a mindset, lifestyle, or culture that you adapt into your habits and practices. Acceptance of a practice "will" become a behavior. Behavior is dictated by what is inside of you. **The fourth level of consciousness states that you must live the laws and live in the laws;** in order to be protected from the threat of depression, anger, and sadness of the traps of life. It is the person that covers their life by these principles that shall experience the happiness and success that they deserve. Remember, "happy is he who **keeps the law**". [Prov 29:18] KJV

This is your new day to live. Today is a day of rejuvenation. Today is your day, it belongs to you. You own this day. Your time is now to rise up and experience the greatest love of all. You being you. You accepting you, but most of all, you loving you. Ah, that is what this has been all about "LOVE". Self-love, Self-evaluation, Self-growth, Self-respect, self-awareness, and time for the development and care of YOU.

Learn to live and be happy, by changing your perceptions of reality. Learn to live and be happy by creating consistent behavior that is governed by following the principles of this book. Learn to live and be happy by understanding the power of the spirit, the training needed for the mind, and the teachings needed for the instability of the heart. Live the life of a champion by loving yourself first and enough to give yourself the courage to live. Tomorrow is not promised, but right now, you and I have the opportunity to be stress-free from the violation of the universal principles that govern this world.

The fourth level of consciousness says **you must "live"** the laws or principles that will make you happy and successful. What does it mean to live something? Breathe something?

Be something? What does it mean to you, to have the opportunity to change your life? **If you change the way you think, you will change the way you live.** Life is short and many people live a long life of not living and living good! Can a person truly live all 100 laws of this order, at the same time? I CAN'T and neither do I find it wise to attempt to either. The secret to living this life is simple and that is finding 10 to 12 things everyday that you do well and do them. It took me almost 33 years to come to the ultimate conclusion of happiness in this life and success within this journey, to know this priceless secret to living a good life today. And that is, If you know you do something well, be conscious of it and just do it. The lie about success has always been taught, that you must achieve an objective, rather than live in the objective. That type of mindset leaves absolutely no room for life's unexpected turns and twists. Neither does it leave room for the first level of consciousness, which says we are all, governed by principles that are beyond this world. If that is the case, then someone other than ourselves has the power to make us go left, when we want to go right. Does that make you a failure; not if you understand the four levels of consciousness? But, our society has promoted the behavior of overachievers. More is better! Bigger is better! Get it done yesterday! Who are you trying to out do? Remember, that happiness has been misconstrued as an outward presentation that is affirmed by people we are exposed to or the people we seek to appreciate our ability to live up to other people's interpretation of what it is and how it should be applied to our lives. To overachieve is to seek affirmation from someone or something. To really achieve happiness or success you just need to be you, no really you, no, I mean the real you.

Don't try to master the universe; it is too complex for you and me. Don't try to be perfect; perfection is only perfect through an honest and sincere heart. What are ten things that you know you do right? What are ten principles from this book that you know you can live day in and day out? Live ten and practice ninety. Live today and learn more tomorrow. Aggressively pursue ten of these laws to take ownership of them and passively learn the other ninety by meditating on their encompass in your life.

CHAPTER 12
The Decree and Declaration Over Your Happiness and Success, STARTS TODAY!

I decree and declare a proclamation of freedom, in your life right now. I speak deliverance from depression, low self-esteem, doubt, fear, disbelief, and limited thinking. I add to your spirit: peace, contentment and wisdom. I take away from you, the inability to believe in yourself and the negative energy that is crippling your future. I LOVE YOU BECAUSE I AM ABLE TO LOVE MYSELF FIRST. I have loved you enough to give you my best in hopes that you will take this piece of doctrine and live happy and be successful. Change is not easy. But change is always needed to live in a new day. I challenge you today. I petition you to wake up and see that the world is bigger than your thoughts and feelings. I petition you to learn what you cannot see, that you know is real and that is the forces, principles and laws of this world that always without a shadow of doubt will have good and bad consequences in your life. **Start** by knowing the first level of consciousness. Yes, you are not your own, you are being governed by forces that are beyond this world. **Second**, make a commitment to know what these forces and principles are. **Third**, teach yourself to respect laws and principles by practicing, educating, and indulging yourself in the desire for a better you through these laws. **Finally**, live in truth. Live what you know you can live. Live in the laws by making them a part of your life. Live the part of the laws that make sense for you today. Be you, but desire to be a better you, before life teaches you the hard way, to be a better you. Change, but change for what is needed in your life today. Separate, but separate what is bringing you up and what is trying to tear you down. Love, but love with purity and freedom of choice, not with selfish ambitions and the need to be accepted. You deserve to be happy and today is the day for you to be happy. Live I say, in "today" and you will never have a need to live in the disappointments of yesterday or the anxieties of tomorrow. Let go, be happy and let your success be measured only by YOU.

Sincerely,
Israel Johnson

References

THE POWER OF THE UNIVERSE

PROVERBS 29:18 KJV

http://www.worldbank.org/depweb/english/modules/enviro nm/water/,

JOHN 4:24 KJV

GENESIS 1:27 KJV